THE OWL

A Photographic Essay

by Manabu Miyazaki

Chronicle Books • San Francisco

First Chronicle Books edition 1990.

Printed in Japan

Library of Congress Cataloging-in-Publication Data

Miyazaki, Manabu, 1949–
    [Mori ni habataku kokō no ōja. English]
    The Owl: A Photographic Essay / Manabu Miyazaki. — First
       chronicle books ed.
     p.   cm.
    Translation of: Mori ni habataku kokō no ōja.
    ISBN 0-87701-803-0
    1. Owls. 2. Owls — Pictorial works.   I. Title.
QL696.S8M5913   1990
598′.97 — dc20   90-2130
                                                  CIP

Editing: Deborah Stone
Cover design: Giorgio Baravalle
Cover photograph: Manabu Miyazaki

Distributed in Canada by Raincoast Books,
112 East Third Avenue, Vancouver, B.C. V5T 1C8

10 9 8 7 6 5 4 3 2 1

Chronicle Books
275 Fifth Street
San Francisco, CA 94103

INTRODUCTION

No bird has the appeal of an owl. Those rounder-than-round eyes framed in an expressive round face draw us close. We sense the owl's wisdom at once. Its body is endearing, an oval of fluffy feathers. And yet, the owl is a bold bird of prey. A nocturnal hunter, its way of life lies hidden by the veil of night.

The more carefully I imagined what that life might be, the more intrigued I grew. I became determined to know this charming bird. I longed to enter its unknown world, to experience the surprise and inspiration I knew I would find there.

I was born and raised in Inatani, a valley in Nagano Prefecture, Japan. Sandwiched between the majestic Southern Alps rising to the east and the austere Central Alps towering to the west, it is the floor under the so-called roof of Japan. Inatani was the classroom where I studied the ways of nature.

The call of the Ural owl was a part of our lives. When darkness fell around us at play, that *hoh-ho horokko hoh-ho* was our signal to go home. Sometimes, complete darkness came before the call. Sometimes it sounded more like *hoh hoh hoh hoh*, but even as a child I knew that voice.

I also remember hearing a piercing *fgyaaa fgyaaa gowa gowa gowa*, but it never occurred to any of us to associate such grating sounds with an owl. Every year during late fall these screams just after sundown would let us know how close at hand was the season of blasting wintry wind. My father would say, "That's a raccoon who has left its young and is wandering around looking for a new home." I never doubted him at the time, but I have since learned that raccoons make no such sound.

The Owl

The owl's outstanding characteristic is undoubtedly its enormous eyes. Big eyes are advantageous for an animal of the night, but the size of an owl's eyes relative to its body is quite striking. Both eyes are situated on the front of its face, so the owl shares with humans the ability to judge an object's distance. The owl makes the greatest possible use of this advantage in hunting. Of equal importance are the oversized ear holes which pick up even the tiniest movements. These sharp eyes and ears can locate prey with great precision.

The owl's amazingly flexible neck enables it to make the most of these senses. With its binocular vision, the owl cannot see to the side or directly behind itself. This problem is solved by its neck, which can turn 180 degrees in both directions, giving the owl 360-degree vision.

Another advantageous feature is the owl's built-in muffler, flight feathers that slice through the air in near silence. Each feather is covered with a velvety sound-suppressing fuzz that makes the sound of an owl's wings hard to hear even on perfectly still evenings.

Most birds have three talons in front and one in back. The owl, however, grasps with four talons, two in front and two in back. It can bring one of the back talons to the front when necessary. The talons are hairy on top, but on the underside the flesh is bumpy to provide good traction. This rough undersurface prevents a caught mouse from wriggling away, and its desperate attempts to bite will yield only a mouthful of hair.

Clearly, the owl is armed with a number of unique adaptive strategies for surviving and hunting in the special world of night, strategies that set it apart in the bird world.

Owls live all over the planet, the greatest variety of species making their home in the northern hemisphere. Humans have a long history of involvement with owls. In ancient China, small saucers of unglazed clay or bronze were cast in the shape of owls, and were used for serving sake on social occasions and for offerings to ancestors. Owls were believed to ward off demons, so owl-shaped carvings were buried with the dead.

In ancient Athens, owls were associated with the goddess of wisdom. According to Greek myth, they were a favorite messenger for the goddess Athena. During Rome's ascendancy Athena became Minerva, but she remained the goddess of craftsmen, a prophetess who made the most of her wisdom and strategic skill to win struggles without resorting to war. Minerva, whose name also means *the thinker*, is associated with academics, prophecy, invention, clarity of thinking, and philosophy. The owl's reputation in the West certainly benefited from its association with these goddesses.

During the Muromachi Period (1392–1573) in Japan, the owl was considered all-powerful, prophetic, and capable of casting out demons. These ideas derive from Buddhist teachings, and temples of that era displayed carvings of various types of owls. The owl continued to be associated with the arts through the Azuchi-Momoyama Period (1573–1598), but during the Edo Period the bird's reputation reversed completely. The owl became reviled as an evil bird and bearer of bad luck. But even during the Edo Period, paper dolls cut in the shape of owls were used as charms to protect against chicken pox and apothecaries kept owls caged in front of their shops to attract customers. During the latter Edo Period, the Haiku poet Issa wrote the following verse: "Spring rain, help the owl break its bad habits."

The owl has continued to be maligned right up to the present. The idea that owls possess supernatural powers lingered down through the ages. Prior to electricity, opportunities to closely observe this nocturnal animal were rare. Much of the aversion felt by people down through the years is undoubtedly rooted in the owl's elusive lifestyle and eerie calls.

On the other hand, the Ainu, a native Japanese race, worship the owl, particularly the eagle owl, as the "god of the forest." For centuries the Ainu have closely watched various species of owls to better understand their ecological role in the unspoiled natural environment of Hokkaido. No doubt their worship of the owl grew directly from their discerning observations.

On Indonesian maps, schools are indicated with an owl mark because the owl is the "god of scholarship." This is undoubtedly a legacy from the long period of Dutch colonization; originally, Indonesians disliked the "ghost bird."

The owl has been variously exalted or loathed at given times and places. This range of emotion demonstrates the extent to which humans feel intrigued by this bird. No bird fascinates us like the owl.

I was driving one evening through a town of widely scattered houses in Inatani, Japan. As I passed a row of large buildings, a large bird flew off a telephone pole right in front of me. The size and wing movements of the bird, seen in the beam of my headlights, told me it was an owl. The large buildings were poultry houses lined up like an apartment complex. Each was brightly lit to keep the chickens awake and increase egg production. It occurred to me that tons of feed was used in those buildings, some of which would end up in the stomachs of gully mice and black rats. The owl's staple food is field mice, and to find them, this owl was willing to venture among human structures near the center of town.

What did this mean? That a new strain of owls had adapted to human structures? If so, I might be able to penetrate the cloak of wooded darkness that has so hampered studies of this animal. If I could find a good observation field, I could watch owls all year round. I began my search.

Owl Valley is located near Nakagawa Village in Nagano Prefecture. Twenty years earlier, I had studied the young-rearing practices of owls in this same valley, and upon returning I found that several of the nests I had observed were still in active use. I also found, however, that the forest surrounding the owl nests had been lumbered and reforested some years back. Reforested areas are full of field mice, but without tall trees to perch on, these make poor hunting areas for owls. The owl's hunting strategy is to alight on top of a tree with a good view and wait for a field mouse or other prey to come along. The young trees now dominating the slopes could not offer the owls the perches essential for their survival.

I decided to bring some dead trees into Owl Valley and stand them up. This proved highly successful. By the third day I found owl traces on all three of the trees I had propped up on the slope. Stuck to branches were needle-thin hairs like those that grow on owls' talons. Encouraged by this start, I began collecting more detailed data. To each of the perch trees I attached a sensor equipped with an electromagnetic counter to give me a rough idea of the nightly use rate for each tree. The higher the number on the counter in the morning, the more the tree had been visited during the night. The counter told me that each tree was visited three to seven times, and that this frequency was uniform throughout the month.

I moved around the valley very carefully, trying to read each sign given by the owls and hoping these clever animals would not dislike me. From the beginning I decided I would only observe them from inside a tiny hut I constructed. All I needed from the hut was to be housed each night, curled up in a sleeping bag, so I made it a small plywood affair of about 10 square feet.

Next I brought electricity to Owl Valley because I needed light in order to observe the owls at night. The distance from the village through the logging road to Owl Valley was almost a mile. After erecting and wiring sixteen electric poles, I ran low wattage through the wires to accustom the owls to dim light. I waited, then raised the illumination slightly and gave them time to accept the stronger lighting. I increased the illumination at regular intervals and after several days the entire valley was lit up every night.

Throughout the lighting process I tried to hide from the owls the fact that a human was behind these changes. The project was large scale, but I was as discreet as possible; the owls demonstrated no misgivings whatsoever about inhabiting a valley now in the vanguard of technology.

Every night I was captivated by new discoveries and surprises. The first year went by quickly. I was so transfixed by the owls, I spent 200 nights in my hut in the valley. After a while, the owls recognized me. When I was taking pictures, though, they ignored me and continued to behave naturally. I was fascinated by these animals that have been so revered by many cultures.

The owl is a bird of prey like the eagle or hawk. During previous research I had observed the nesting behavior of all sixteen species of eagles and hawks inhabiting Japan. All were fierce and fascinating; each species and each individual had its own character and personality. Tracking birds of prey was fascinating because of the opportunity to observe these separate personalities up close and respond accordingly. When I made these birds the objects of my study, however, I saw that the more absorbed I became in them, the more wary of me they became. The more I tracked eagles and hawks, the more they read my actions and hid from me the behaviors I wanted to see. On the other hand, when I was eating, reading, napping, or listening to the radio, they paraded their lives in front of me. As soon as I understood this, I did all I could to ease their anxiety.

Later, when I began observing the owls in the valley, I employed from the start the strategy of affected unconcern I had developed in my earlier studies. When it was appropriate to be discreet, I was the soul of circumspection, but when I was not attending to them I moved about brazenly. When I shut myself up in the hut, I was elaborately unconcerned with whether owls appeared or not. Nothing could have hurt my purposes more than to show an intense and expectant face at the window, my eyes darting around to catch every movement. Therefore, my tent life was a lackadaisical round of reading, drinking sake, and napping.

Of course, without the assurance that my sensors were picking up each and every owl visiting my trees, I probably could not have managed such a nonchalant attitude. When I heard the sound *pi pi pi pi*, a bird had alighted on the left perch. When it was the right perch I heard *bi bi bi bi*; *bu bu bu bu* meant an owl had landed on the middle perch. At each of these sounds I would look out the appropriate window to see the bird on the appropriate perch.

On the face of it, my methods might appear shamefully lazy, but my technique was developed through long experience. Almost no wildlife today completely rejects human structures. Such structures have inundated the natural world so much that animals have become accustomed to them. Daily experience teaches wildlife which human structures pose a threat. I decided to take advantage of this tolerance to employ advanced technology to the maximum extent and what my fancy machines could not tell me, I would seek through traditional methods of direct observation.

Three years passed. The owls came to Owl Valley every day. They raised their young there. Knowing full well I sat in my little observation hut, the families still never hesitated to show themselves. They had carefully evaluated me and judged me safe, provided I maintained a certain distance.

Awesome Appetites

Autumn is the season of intense hunting for the owl. Japan has four distinct seasons, and since the owl does not migrate to escape winter, the autumn catch is critical to the survival of each individual and the propagation of the entire species. In autumn the owl is continually ravenous. Gobbling one field mouse after another every night makes no dent in the bird's voracity. A single owl might catch ten field mice in one night. If it finds a fruitful hunting ground, twenty. The mice weigh about an ounce each. The owl swallows them whole, storing their energy for later use. I was amazed to observe that the owl's insatiable appetite flourished from late September until mid-November.

Each animal, owl and field mouse, bets its life on its strategies for lasting the winter. Field mice spend the winter in underground tunnels safe from predators. The food they store in these tunnels must last through the winter, so they apply themselves diligently to gathering great quantities of tree seeds, grass seeds, and insect chitin from late summer through early fall. Apprehension over the inexorable approach of winter strongly motivates mice in the wild to gather as much as they can. All day, every day, they are bent on their task.

Fall is the time of harvest. No other season shows so clearly the workings of the food chain. Plants, in order to survive the winter, ripen and release their seeds all at once. Mice gathering those seeds are spied by owls, who then commence the hunt. The owl's staple food is the field mouse, and in the fall, more scurry about than at any other time. The number of mice a female owl is able to eat in the fall determines the number of eggs she will lay the following spring. In other words, finding those places where field mice gather in the fall determines whether or not these owls will breed successfully the following year. Land containing many plants with high seed production attract mice; owls with a number of such locations within their territories will bear many offspring. (One year I fed extra mice by hand to one owl. The next spring her egg production doubled from two to four. After the eggs hatched, however, she failed to catch enough mice to feed them all, and one or two died.)

Many mice escape the owls' clutches and survive the winter. The survivors and the owls enter their breeding seasons concurrently in the spring. The owl begins nightly patrols of the same hunting grounds that yielded such good results the previous fall. It finds the offspring of the autumn survivors and feeds them to its own young. Thus, the owl's success is also determined by the number of individual mice that survived through the fall and winter.

Fall is also the season when the young adult birds leave their parents. In fact, offspring, father, and mother all live and hunt separately during this time. First, the young owls take leave of their parents who have been cooperating since spring to raise them. In Owl Valley this happens in mid-September. At this point the trees are still lush with green leaves and the days are hot, but the night air belongs to autumn. The only song is the chirping of crickets in the grass. When the crickets stop, the silence is almost frightening. The owls glide soundlessly about the valley looking for a perch. The rule is, the early bird gets the perch, and in the competition for mice, the advantage goes to the owl whose perch commands the better view. The young owls who have just left the nest will naturally be attracted to these trees, and so will their parents. Thus, the best trees are never bare of owls.

Young owls are lazy. They often monopolize a branch for thirty minutes to an hour, waiting for likely prey. Sometimes other owls scare these perch "hogs" away by flinging themselves through the air at them like arrows. These experiences traumatize the naive young owls severely. Having to watch for attackers on all sides distracts them from the hunt. This anxiety keeps young owls from enjoying much success at first.

The owl hurling itself at a young bird may well be its mother or father or a sibling. Parents consider this flinging attack a matter of course and go about it with great conviction. The young owls, however, after being assaulted even by family members, begin to lose their trust.

The silent fall nights are suddenly ripped apart by the most strident screams, unearthly sounds that only the experienced observer knows to connect with an owl. Truly an uncanny, penetrating noise—*goh goh goh goh goaaa goh goaaa goh goaaa goh goyah goyah goyah goyah*—that sound vibrates to the pit of human stomachs and stands our hair on end. For thirty years that sound had been a question mark, a puzzle in my mind. Living in Owl Valley finally unraveled the puzzle.

The female owl is behind the harrowing screech, which is heard only from mid to late fall. It is the call she makes when, facing winter, she seeks solitude. After the female has given her young their independence, she evidently needs to separate from her mate as well. Her family is a nuisance and she wants to be alone. The female does her own hunting during this season of plentiful prey. Fall is, in fact, the only season when she can hunt for herself, so the piercing scream reverberates through the valley only in fall. As long as she keeps it up, neither her mate nor her children will approach her.

Around mid to late October, the young owls disappear. They leave Owl Valley to search for new homes. The sight of young owls flitting back and forth in the September sky is gone. The newly solitary female parent searches for food. She is desperately hungry. Females monopolize the branches of Owl Valley's several perch trees almost all night. After a while, however, the male begins to put in an appearance. No longer does the female relentlessly drive him off, but she uses the scream to keep him at a safe distance.

Meanwhile, autumn marches on. Every day fall colors grow deeper and the nights colder. The female's hysterical shriek is apt to be answered by the male's call. His *hoh-ho horokko hoh-ho* coming from the forest sounds like an effort to soothe her. Moreover, the female's shriek has somehow lost its punch.

The female finally eats her fill of field mice and is satisfied. Fall's adamant repelling of the male gives way to a new attitude. With ample stored nourishment to provide her body's energy, her drive to hunt falls off markedly. At this point fall colors are fading and winter birds such as the thrush and hawk become conspicuous.

Winter—Season of Love

During the last half of November, though the female's appetite has abated, she still consumes one or two field mice per night. When she spies a good chance she takes it, but she is no longer a zealous stalker. Presumably her stored energy is already being used, enabling her to survive on less. At the same time, fewer prey are available, and those that remain are adept at eluding the hunt; they are not likely to be caught by a heavy female who has been eating well all autumn.

Various phenomena characteristic of this season, such as changes in the availability of prey, arouse subtle changes within the body of the female. Her declining interest in the hunt accompanies an increased reliance on her mate's hunting prowess. The frenzied need to repel him is gone. The ferocious *goh goh goaaa goaaa* turns to a coaxing *boa boa*—sweet-talk asking for food.

Having also spent the fall concentrating on his stomach's needs, the male too is somewhat heavier than usual, but he hunts as vigorously as ever. The prey dart about more quickly than in early fall, but this only whets his appetite for the game. This contest sharpens his responses and feeds his self-confidence. His pride at being a skilled hunter with a kept female is perhaps the reason he waxes in stature during this season to become "king of the forest." His *hoh-ho horokko hoh-ho* rings through the forest more and more, until it fills the night. The female responds immediately with her wheedling cry.

The male varies his call slightly according to whether he is calling the female or telling her where he is. When he wants to tell her or other males his location, he elongates and stresses the final *ho* to produce a tremolo. When he wants to call the female, the final sound is lowered and cut off. He has other variations as well, such as stressing the first *hoh-ho* or stretching it out. Clearly, each variation has meaning.

By the time the night forest is full of these male and female voices, the pairs are moving toward intimacy. The night forest conceals the exact movements of its creatures, so these calls and responses must impart a great deal of information about the caller's whereabouts and activities. They also distinguish males from females.

During this period, the male's main pattern of activity involves far-ranging forays into the forest in a circle around the nest. The radius of his movements is about a mile in any direction, while the female's radius is only about one-quarter of a mile. The female typically loiters near the nest. When the male announces that he has brought more food, she tells him where she is with an intermittent *boaaa boaaa boaaa*. Then he approaches with the prey. His call may come from far away, but even at one-half mile it is perfectly audible to humans. The female's voice, except for her autumn scream, is harder to hear. Her voice is perfectly audible to the male owl, however. If she answers at all he leaps to her side.

As winter settles in, the female depends more and more on the male for food. She waits in the severe cold, unsure of her next meal, losing strength every day. The depletion of her stored energy weakens her, thus increasing her dependency. This utter reliance on the male shifts dominance to his side.

The male announces his location often, even when he is hunting. This not only briefs his mate, but informs other males that he has a mate to come home to and a nest site he is preparing for breeding. Other males hear him and respond. These may be unbonded males or those claiming another territory. Generally, male owls will not approach another's nest area but will listen and respond from a distance. Because males cover a wide area to get food, their territories tend to overlap.

December passes by, and by January male territorial competition gathers momentum. Added to the usual *hoh-ho horokko hoh-ho* is a new male call: *ho-ho-ho-ho-ho-ho*. Every day around twilight the male fills the air around his nest with this laughlike hoot. It informs outsiders that his nest site is now determined, so the call is long, deep, and tenacious.

This call signals the advent of copulation. When the male brings his gifts to the female, his urgent call echoes deep into the wintry forest night. Intent on the prey he clutches, the female presents herself fully as she sidles up to him. For awhile they coo to each other in the tones of a mutually recognized ardor. Then the male's *pi pi pi pi pi pi* announces that he has accepted the female's love. As winter stars twinkle over a forest undisturbed by even a breath of wind, the owls mate. During this period, which lasts almost a month, the couples copulate about three times a night.

Nature's profound wisdom is manifest by the owls mating in winter. The bulging stomachs of fall have been depleted. In nature female fertility is commonly at its peak when winter assails the body. If we researched the optimum time for owls to breed, we would find winter the only season they actually have time for it. If owls did not breed in winter, the warmer seasons would be too short for egg-laying, incubating, and young-rearing.

Secrets of the Tree Hole

As winter tightens its icy grip on the forest, the male owl keeps up a frantic pace—copulating, building the nest, and hunting. It is his most fulfilling season, but it also puts his life on the line. My photographic skills were severely taxed during this time, too. For one thing, I was determined to learn what owls do in their nest holes. Humans have only been able to guess at their habits; no one has ever observed owls in their nests. Since my primary interest as a photographer is to seek out unknown worlds, over the years I have honed my photographic skills. One inevitable outcome of this search is the use of high-tech equipment. If I could not film my subject, the owl, in all its daily routines, my efforts in Owl Valley would be meaningless.

I knew that every year a brood of owlets was raised in a huge red pine on the upper slopes of Owl Valley. I also knew that the tree was not in use at any other time. In fact, during nonbreeding seasons the owls appeared completely indifferent to it. This allowed me to tinker with the tree openly. The nest was about 200 yards from my observation hut. My plan was to connect a video camera in the tree to a monitor in the hut so that I could pick up all the activity in the hole. I also intended to install a still camera in the hole and operate it from the hut by remote control. That way I could photograph the owls without frightening them. I had to set all of this up before nesting season began.

The large red tree had a hole perfectly situated for peering into the nest. By installing a camera in the hole I could photograph the eggs and the growth of the owlets. I also intended to record their activities through the lens of a special camera preloaded with 750 exposures. I needed such long film so I would not have to interfere during the three months of nest preparation, incubation, and young-rearing. With 36-exposure film, I would always be showing up at the hole to change the film, frightening the birds in the process.

I had to anticipate every conceivable weather condition and thoroughly protect the equipment from the beginning. I protected both cameras from rains and temperature fluctuations with waterproof housing. The housing also helped muffle the sound of the shutter.

I also installed a parabolic reflecting microphone in the hole and a sensor to alert me in the hut if any creature approached the vicinity of the nest. I also had a buzzer that sounded whenever the owls entered or left the nest. The cables carrying all this information spanned 185 yards. With these added to my lighting cables, I had stretched almost three miles of wire over Owl Valley.

The pair of owls that had been in the forest passing prey from beak to beak and copulating through the first part of winter suddenly appeared at the nest in early February. The male perched at the entrance and called *bo bo bo bo bo bo*. Nearby, the female responded with her cry of *goaa goaa goaa*. The monitor speaker in the hut relayed this so clearly I could have been in the nest with them. Only the male appeared on the video monitor. As I watched I noticed that he didn't open his mouth to call; instead he made the sound resonate by swelling his throat up like a balloon. I had never suspected this surprising way of calling.

Presently the male flew into the hole. Bits of wood were piled up near the entrance from previous years of nesting there. He lay on his stomach on the pile and began to dig. Though his body trembled with the effort, he still managed to cry *bo bo bo bo bo bo*. For one or two hours a night, the male would dig and call, stop, dig, and call again. During his breaks, he took off hunting. When he returned with the prey, his *hoh-ho horokko hoh-ho* to his mate would resound through the valley. After delivering the animal to her, he again closeted himself in the hole, digging and singing. His cries seemed to be reassuring his mate that he was hard at work on the nest. The female sat on a branch between 50 and 100 yards away, listening and eating her food. Sometimes her low cry, a gravelly *foogo foogo foogo*, the sound of deep satisfaction, traveled by microphone all the way to the hut. After listening to the male singing in the hole for some time, I would suddenly realize he was gone, then discover him copulating with his mate. This pattern continued for about twenty days.

Inside the hole the male dug out a saucer-shaped depression. The resulting depression was a nest that had required no building materials. After the work was finished, the female came and sat in the nest. Until then she had only come as far as the entrance to see how the work was proceeding.

The Female Raises the Young

When the female moved into the hole to prepare for egg-laying, the male's work was done. He came and went from the nest less frequently; she planted herself in it more and more firmly. The male hunted, passed her the prey, and spent hours calling *ho ho ho ho ho* from a high perch on the red pine. A few days later, sometime in early March, the female laid a round white egg a little bigger than a ping pong ball. Over a period of five days she laid three more. For a while, the first two lay neglected where they rolled, but after laying the third the female conscientiously began to sit on them. From that point on, the nest became her exclusive domain.

For one month, the image on my monitor was of the female settled in her incubating posture. Yet, every time I looked at her I made a new discovery. She was remarkably busy, constantly shifting her position and turning the eggs with her beak to distribute her body heat. The big eyes so characteristic of the owl were evidently unnecessary in the hole, for she usually kept them closed, as if napping. Her eyes drooped to mere slits, and she sometimes nibbled on the inner walls of the tree or broke up bits of wood or dirt in her beak, as if to break the monotony. On more than a few occasions she sat on her charges for twenty-four hours without food or drink. Outside, the male called *hoh-ho horokko hoh-ho* to encourage her. She responded with a weak *foogo foogo*.

The microphone connected to the monitor was another source of discovery. Despite her bored appearance, the female's ears picked up important information. The owl's ear holes, hidden under a cloak of feathers, are quite large relative to the rest of its body, and their acute sensitivity benefits the owl in a number of ways. I have already mentioned how the owl's hearing helps in the hunt. In Owl Valley I learned that the ears also enable the owl to distinguish and analyze each sound coming through the forest.

Before I heard for myself the sounds picked up by the microphone, it had never occurred to me that the nest hole is itself an excellent sound-collecting mechanism. Even tiny sounds that escape humans came across distinctly through the microphone. For example, a radio playing in a house nearly a mile away was perfectly audible. On my own, even on quiet, windless nights, I never heard this radio once. The barking of dogs in the distance came through as well.

When animals passed through the undergrowth near the nest hole, the mike picked up their rustling. I heard the *thump thump* of a rabbit, and even the gliding steps of the fox. The animals' location and distance from the tree hole was also clear. I was amazed. Obviously, the owl, too, analyzed these sounds to determine each creature's distance.

One day people gathering edible mountain plants came into the valley. I had not noticed them, but suddenly their voices came over the speaker as they neared the owl's hole. I wondered what the owl would do. My eyes glued to the monitor, I watched her every movement. She snapped out of her napping pose to ascertain, with wide-open eyes, the intruders' location. From 100 yards away, they approached to about 50 yards before heading off in another direction. At 50 yards, the female appeared tense and dead still on the monitor. Her feathers were pulled in tight as she analyzed the information supplied by the sounds. As the sounds receded, her feathers fluffed out again and the fire of alarm faded from her eyes. Soon she fell back into her napping pose.

The Mother and Her Eggs Converse

The microphone in the tree hole led me to yet another discovery. Around the twentieth day of incubation the female occasionally began to call *goh goh goh goh goh goh*. I had never heard an owl make this sound. It resembled a weak fit of coughing, but sounded more like a murmur of encouragement. She often murmured like this when turning her eggs, and over the next few days I became accustomed to it. After some time I began to hear through the microphone a faint *bifee bifee*.

> *Goh goh goh goh goh goh.*
> *Bifee.*
> *Goh goh gof goh goh goh.*
> *Bifee.*

From the twenty-fifth or twenty-sixth day of incubation, the female's call was consistently followed by cries of *bifee*. I was amazed to realize that these sounds were coming from the unborn owlets. The chicks and their mother were conversing. I had no idea that owls carried on like this, and without the microphone and monitor I never would have known about it.

Four or five days later, the chicks hatched. Throughout their conversation with their mother, they had been knocking the file-like tips of their upper beaks against the inner wall of the egg, struggling to hatch themselves. Their mother had been cheering them on. Hatching requires a mammoth effort, a pattern of rest, knock, and rest again as each chick pecks a crack around the egg's equator. This is why a brood of chicks generally are not born in a single day but break through over a period of two to four days, spurred on by maternal cooing.

The strenuous efforts by the chicks greatly stimulate the female's mothering instinct as the chicks she has single-mindedly, unwaveringly kept warm for thirty days spring to life. She has already read the various signs telling her that life is brewing inside the eggs cradled under her chest. When the knocking comes, she recognizes it as a response to her labor and her mothering instinct awakens.

After the chicks hatch, the mother-child dialogue continues. The mother frequently urges the chicks to accept her food with the cry, *goh goh goh goh goh goh*. Later I came to understand that the chicks' response, *bifee*, expresses the feeling of security. Later the cry develops into *bifeefeefee bifeefeefee*. When the

chicks have eaten their fill of mouse meat torn up and fed to them by their mother and are ready for sleep, that cry comes in full force. This sort of mother-chick behavior may apply not just to owls but to all birds.

The chicks were born in early April and spent roughly thirty days in the nest before flying away. For the first fifteen days, their mother cradled them protectively under her chest while their father continued to hunt and bring the prey to the nest. His typical catch was field mice, but occasionally he would bring a mole, a small bird, or a frog. On average he brought home some sort of bounty six to eight times a night. The mother would take the animal into the nest, prepare it for consumption by tiny mouths, and distribute the pieces. This parental teamwork enabled the offspring to grow quickly. When they were about the size of quails, their plumage began to fill out. Snuggling together usually generated enough body heat to keep the owlets warm, so the mother stopped cradling them except on chilly nights. She took to standing guard in a neighboring tree, entering the hole only to feed the owlets. From nearby she continued to listen to her babies talk in the nest.

They cried *piju piju* when they wanted food or warmth—in other words, when they wanted their mother. This *piju* was their basic cry while they were in the nest. The cry would be strong or weak, or alternate between the two. Each time I looked at the monitor the chicks would be peeping with great gusto, even when they were alone. When not being fed they preened their feathers, flapped their wings, stretched, or slept. I had the impression they cried constantly whenever they were awake, but it may have only seemed that way because there were so many of them.

Variation in the chicks' size was particularly pronounced for the first fifteen days. This was partly because the four owlets hatched over a period of five days; those who hatched first ate for two or three days before their siblings were born. Therefore, at fifteen days the bigger chicks were one and a half times as big as the smaller ones. This can have serious consequences for some broods. If the father is a poor hunter, the food will not make it around to the smaller chicks, and some will die. Fortunately, the father of these owlets was a skilled hunter, and all four chicks were able to grow up and fly away. Two left thirty-one days after hatching, another left three days later, and the last flew out the day after that.

The young owls left the nest in early May. Each chose a branch to perch on to wait for the food its parents would bring. By this time noticeable differences in size had disappeared. Covered in thick plumage, the owlets were in a most appealing stage. They were big enough to eat pygmy and other small mice whole, head first. All the parents had to do was to get the prey to the branches where their offspring perched. The mother had joined the father in the hunt, though she confined her hunting to within 500 to 600 yards of the nest.

The owlets continued to call *piju piju* for food. Once out of the nest, they were amazingly energetic. Flying within a 100-yard radius of the nest, the frisky birds gathered along the routes their parents commonly used when returning with food. Without fully mature wing feathers, the young owls managed to fly using their legs to bound from branch to branch and spreading their wings for balance. To avoid their annoying clamor, the parents went off to hunt silently, without revealing their location.

By June or July, the young owls were excellent flyers. Calling *pichu* instead of *piju*, they flew all around Owl Valley. Their father was the better hunter, so the more energetic young owls shadowed him closely. Because of the racket now accompanying his hunts, his catch began to fall off toward August, but this made the young ones stick to him more closely. They followed him farther to the hunting grounds, which broadened their range of activity.

Again I was in awe at the synchrony in nature. Just as the young owls learned to hunt, various large insects began to proliferate in the forest. The young owls, roaming in pursuit of their father, encountered praying mantises and grasshoppers. After watching their father catch these, the young owls shifted from watching to hunting on their own. Their successes taught them the feel of the hunt. August is the best time for young owls to learn to hunt for themselves because the abundance of insects gives them ample, relatively easy experience.

In August, a hush fell on the valley. The owls were still active, as I could tell from the indigestible remains of their prey I found in the forest, but they no longer called to each other. The owlets no longer cried *pichu* for food or warmth; they were now on their own and had ceased to depend on their parents.

Mysterious Bird of Prey

A nocturnal hunter, much of the owl's way of life is hidden by darkness.

A solitary owl perches on the stump of a dead tree. Old or dead trees are essential for owls, who use them as observation lookouts while hunting.

Perched owls move their heads continually,
scanning for prey with super-sharp eyes and ears.

▶ With prey in view the owl moves swiftly, its flight
sudden and soundless.

Flying thirty feet per second, the owl's usually invisible wing movements are revealed here by eight strobe exposures per second.

In the split second prior to capture, the owl closes
its precious eyes to protect them.

By the time the prey is subdued, the owl's eyes are
open again.

Notice how this owl's left and right wings balance smoothly during the short battle before the prey is firmly clenched.

The owl hovers, searching the weeds for prey.

▶ On spotting prey among the grasses, the owl beats its wings hard and descends.

◄ Its prey taken, the owl glances about as it strangles its victim.

To facilitate leaping into the air, the owl's powerful legs push hard against the earth.

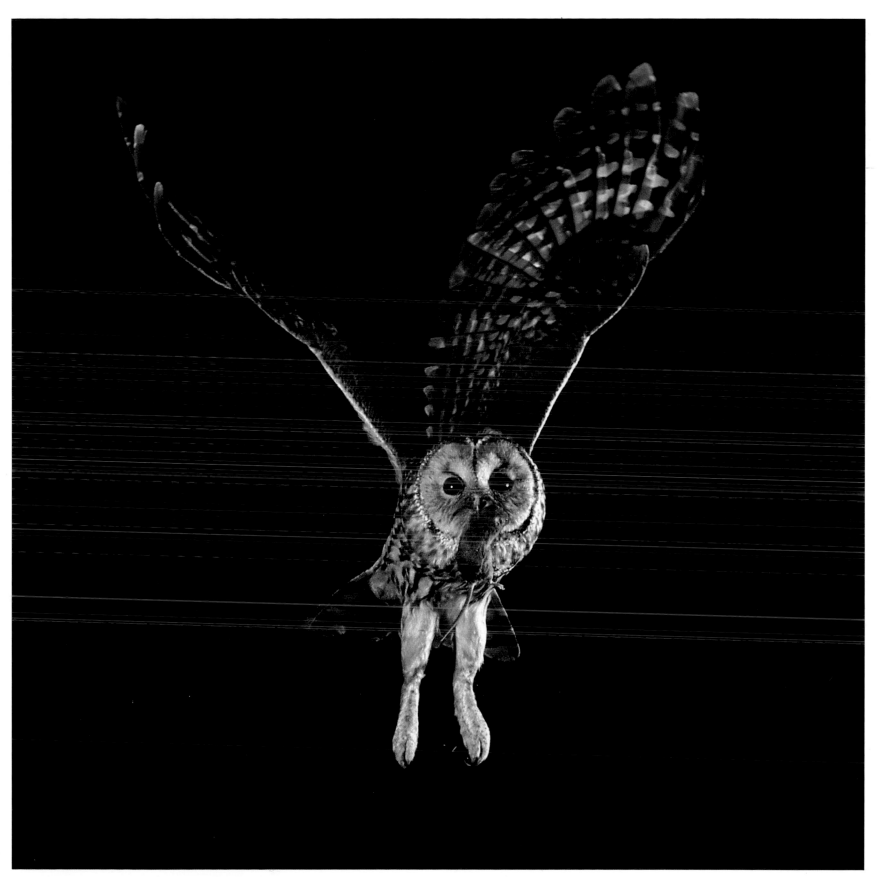

An owl leaps straight up and opens its wings as it
flies off with the kill.

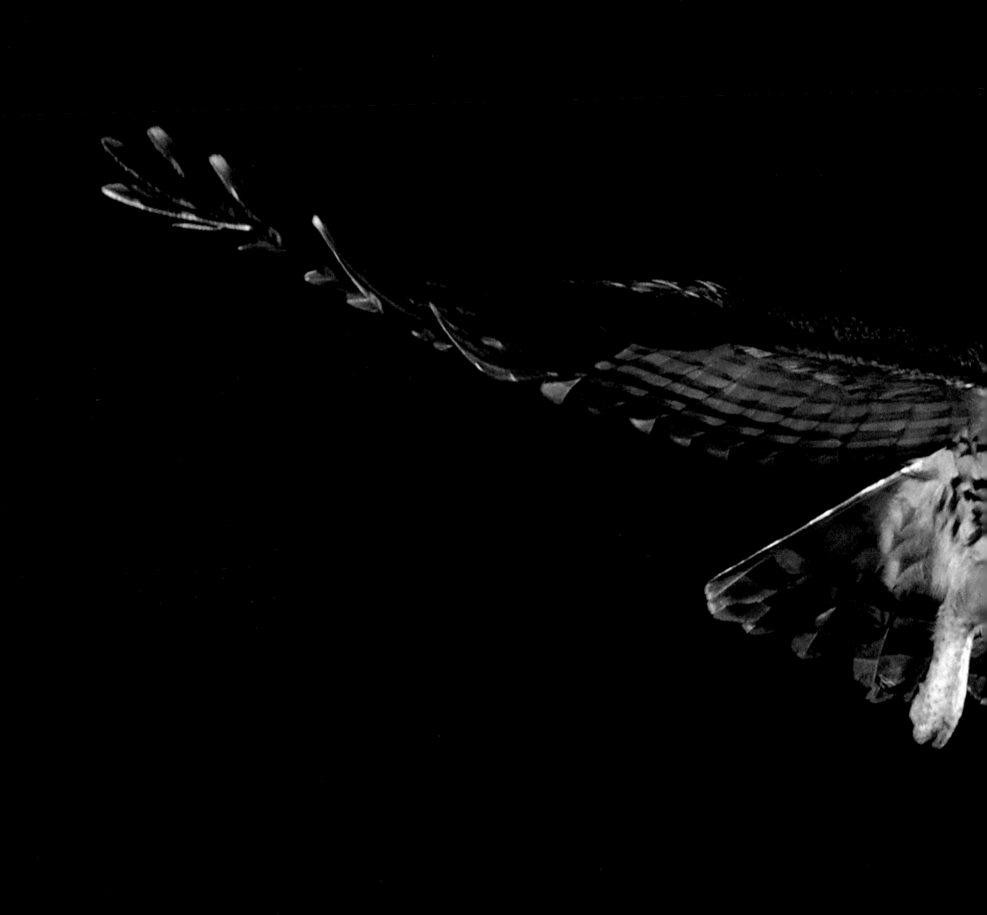

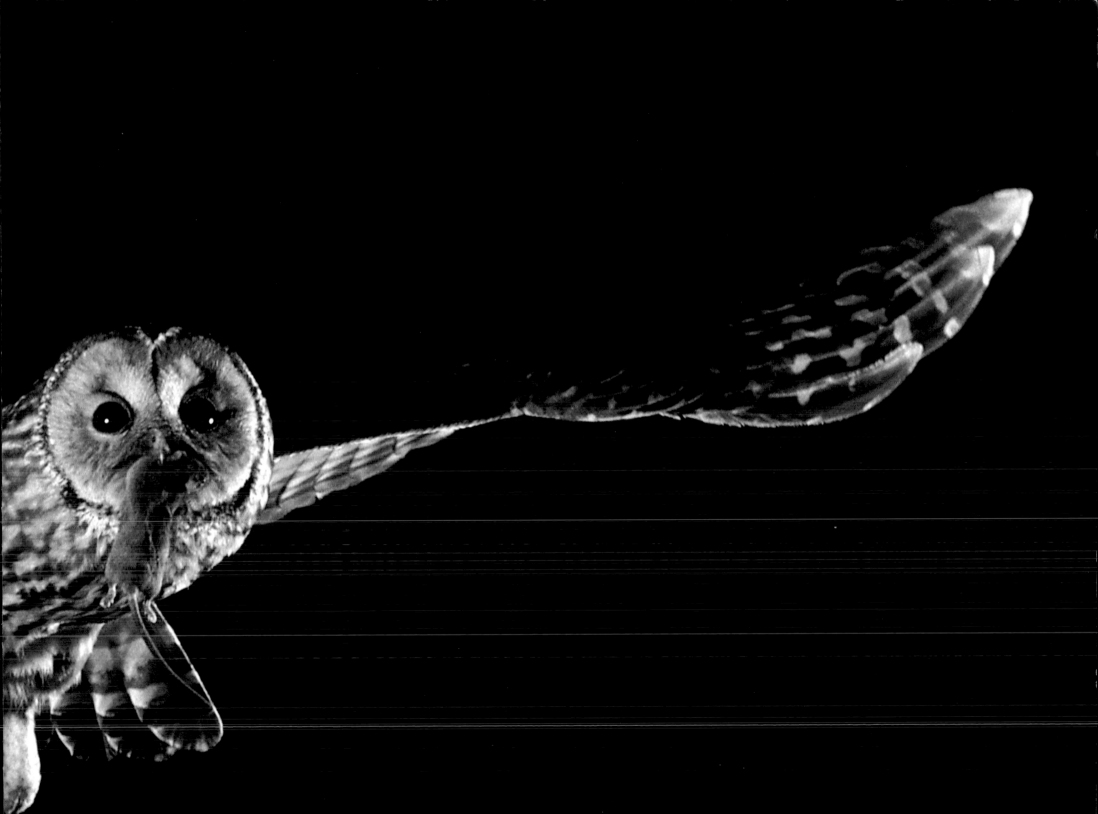

The owl's astonishing night vision guides it precisely, however deep the darkness.

◄ Notice the fine hairs fringing the owl's wing feathers. These hairs silence the owl's flight, making it nearly soundless even on perfectly still nights.

► The owl takes its prey to a safe perch, then prepares it for eating.

The mother returns with prey to the waiting owlets. Though her flight is silent, the owlets know when she nears the nest.

◄ This owl soars through the night forest, heading for her tree hole and her owlets.

► Gliding down toward the nest, owls bring prey to their offspring many times each night.

Large prey, like this bamboo pheasant, is carried in
the owl's talons.

Smaller prey is carried in the beak.

An owlet peers from the nest hole after working its way out of the nest with its feet and beak.

◄ Owlets swallow prey this size whole.

A female sits on her eggs. The eggs, laid in March, are incubated by the female alone. While in the nest, she usually keeps her eyes closed.

▶ The male brings food to the brooding female. The division of labor between them is equal. When the male brings food, the female calls a happy-sounding greeting.

The female shifts her position on the eggs and turns them constantly to make sure her body heat is distributed evenly. Last year's egg shells are scattered nearby.

Male and female are seldom in the nest together. The female lays the eggs on the floor about 1 yard down from the hole's opening.

The owlet plants its legs firmly and stretches. Gradually, wing exercises grow more conspicuous and the nest hole more confining.

▶ The female feeds her brood; rat heads and other delicacies the owlets find hard to eat, she tears to bite-sized bits.

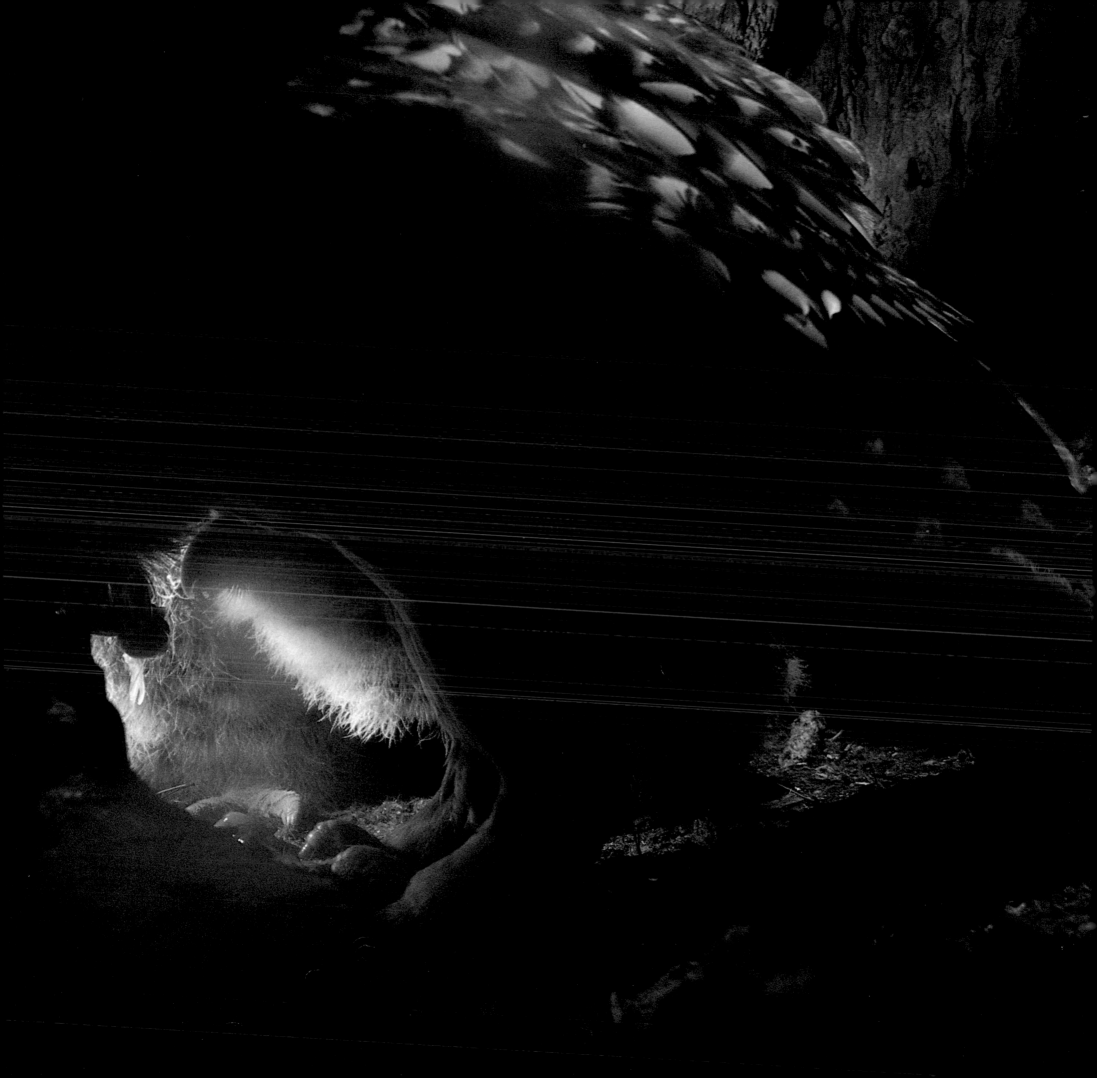

This owlet is nearly ready to leave the nest. Its countenance is lovable, but its fierce nature is already visible.

◄ The rapidly growing owlet, with its mother,
needs the food its father delivers frequently.

The first egg hatches; one month later, the last owlet departs.

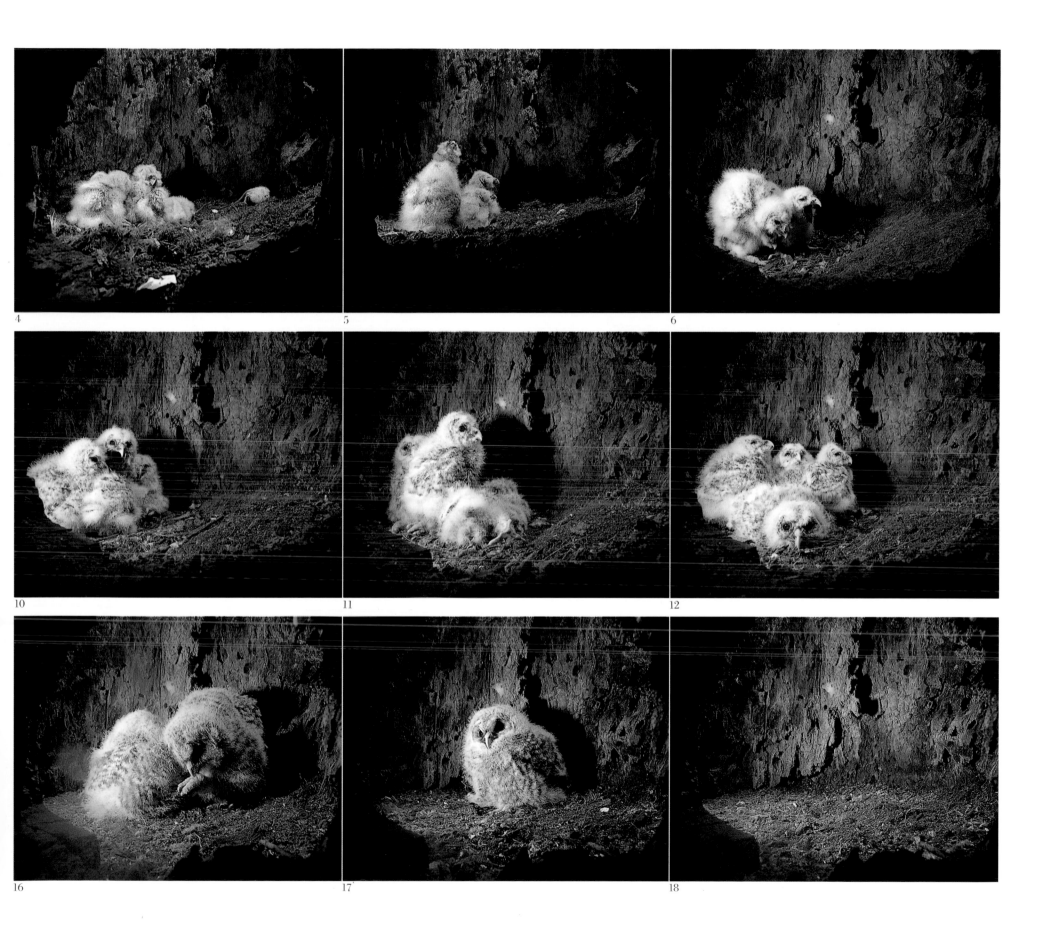

In the late afternoon, a hungry owlet waits for its parents at the nest's entrance.

▶ The owl uses its strong legs to walk straight up the tree; wings are spread for balance.

Spring Brings New Life to the Forest

**Barely a month old, the owlets emerge from the nest in late spring.
Within days they will be ready to fly on their own.**

During the day, this owlet hides behind a wide trunk, attending to every movement, full of curiosity.

► Sometimes the owlets sit completely still, as if imitating a burl on the tree.

These owlets cluster near the nest hole. Once they leave the nest, they are nearly impossible to find. The white fuzz still clinging to their feathers somehow does not expose them against the green hues of spring and summer.

Owlets snuggling together a moment ago are now scrapping. Gradually the distance between them grows.

◄ After leaving the nest, siblings stay together a
mere one or two days. Each quickly begins to
make its own way.

53

This owlet, now on its own, grows bolder daily.

◄ A parent sleeps during the day in the forest. A mixed flock of chickadees, long-tailed titmice, and woodpeckers flitting through the forest chorus a warning.

In July a young adult appeared on a branch often used by both generations. The downy fuzz had vanished, revealing a fine young owl.

▶ Three young adults follow their parents on the hunt. This was the only time I saw the three together.

◄ Even as summer ends, the parents remain in Owl Valley, darting swiftly from perch to perch in search of prey.

► Seen in flight at the instant before alighting, the owl will momentarily shut its lids and nictitating membrane to protect its eyes.

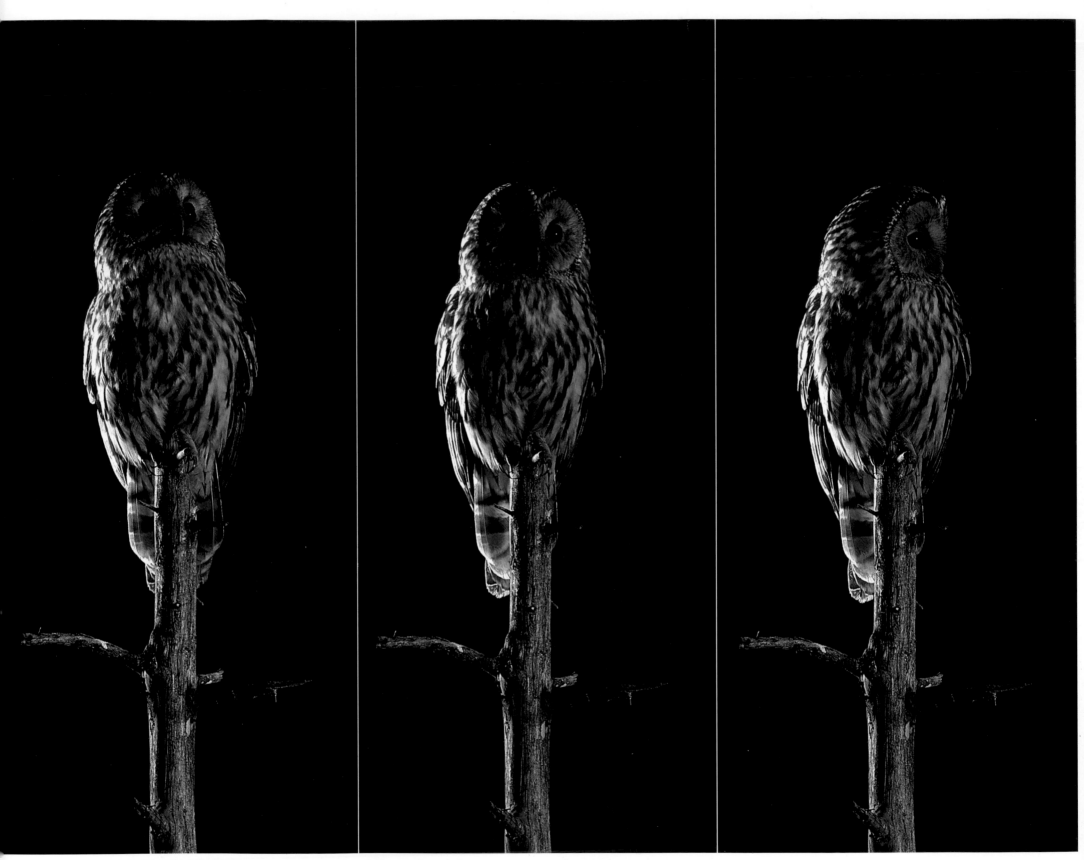

Scanning for prey from its perch, the owl makes full use of its ability to rotate its neck 180 degrees in either direction.

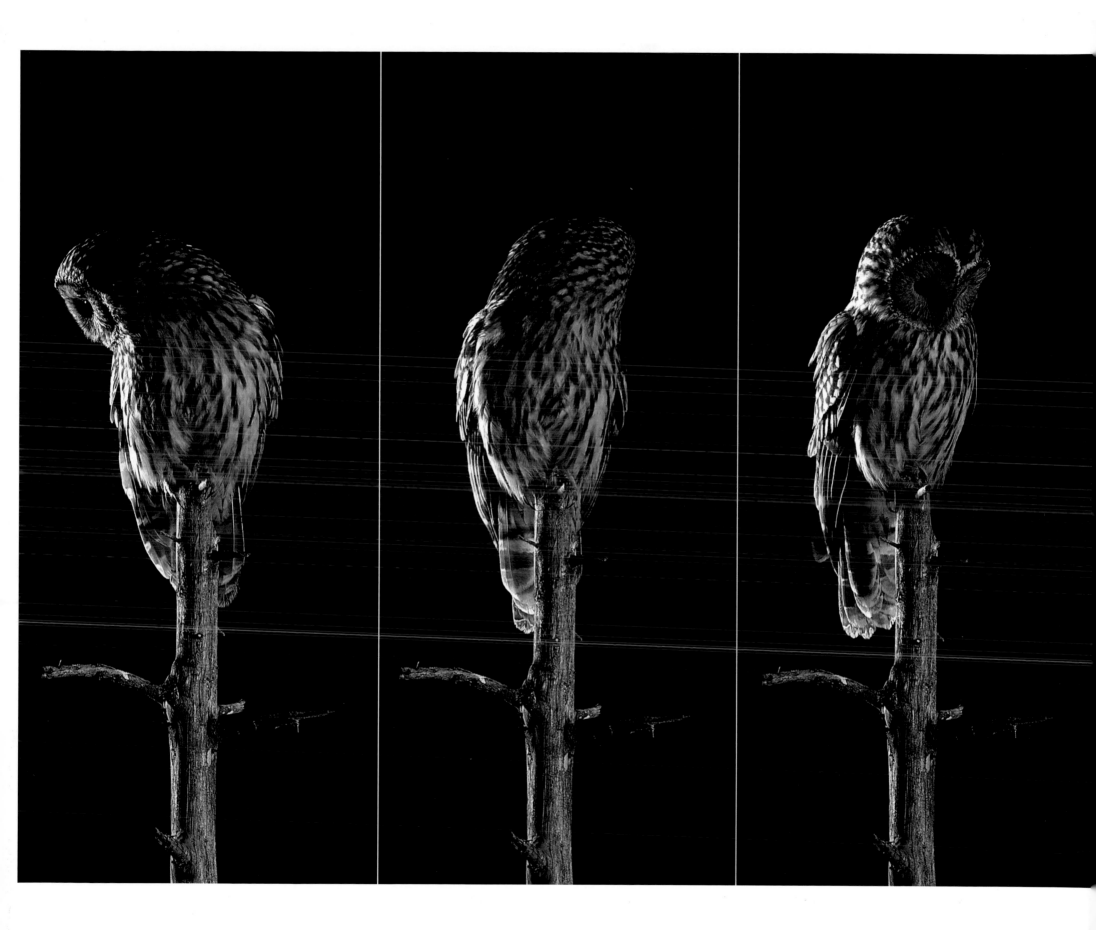

A pigeon is killed and eaten on the spot. Owls do not remove the feathers before eating, as do most other birds of prey.

This same owl returned the next two nights to finish the pigeon.

On still, windless nights, owls will hunt during a light snowfall. They may perch on one tree for an hour or more.

◄ The look of an owl at its dinner; a single meal can take a leisurely two hours.

Owls rarely venture out during heavy snows like this. This bird appeared for an hour at 7:00 P.M.

However heavy the snowfall, the owls go about their late-night business as soon as the snow lets up.

A powdery snow fell for two hours. This owl hunted on through the gentle flakes, but with little success.

Owl and snow go together
beautifully.

Owls are quite active on clear nights, regardless of the temperature, which on this occasion was quite bitter.

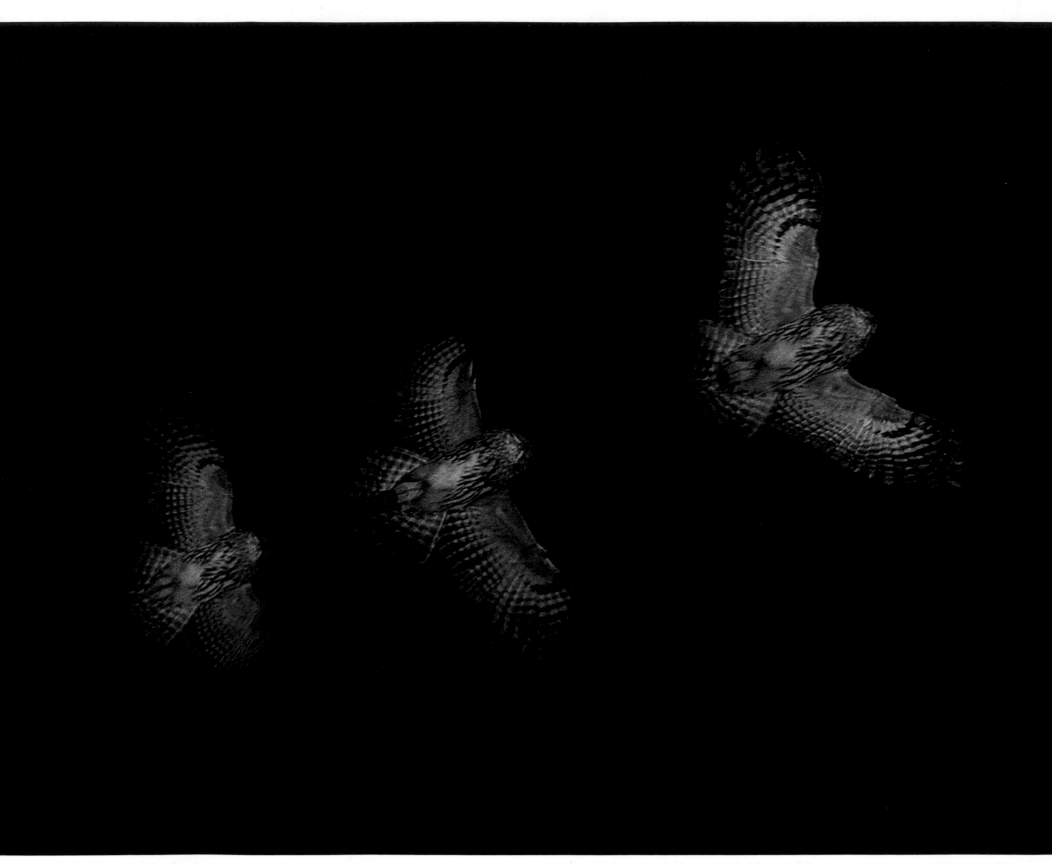

This owl glides slowly at a mere ten feet per second.

▶ A new owl family resides in the hole in this blossoming cherry tree. The same pair has raised offspring in this tree every year for nine years.

The male glides down to the female from high in the sky to copulate.

◄ During the courtship ritual, the female owl sits on a branch about 100 yards from the nest. When her mate brings prey, she calls to him coaxingly and he passes the animal to her.

A male and female perch on the branch of a dead tree at the start of a new mating season.